U.S. Department of Justice
Office of Justice Programs
National Institute of Justice

I0476924

JAN.

07

NIJ

Special **REPORT**

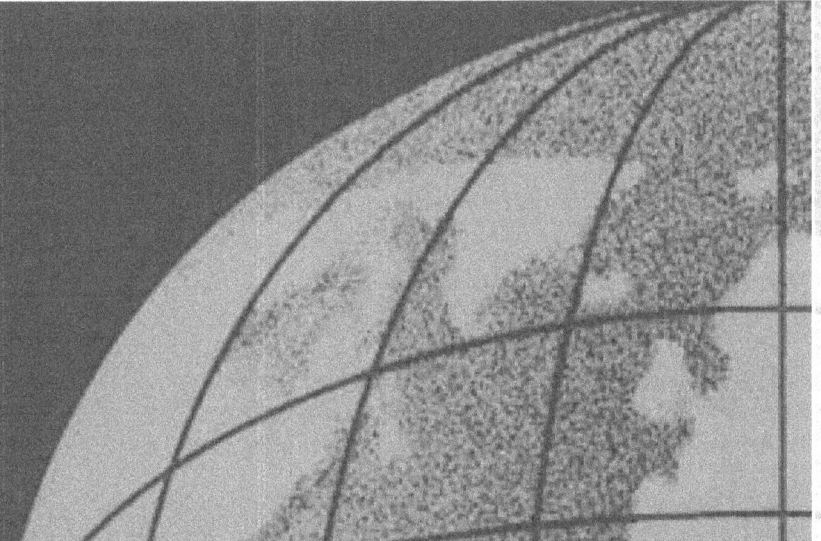

Asian Transnational Organized Crime and Its Impact on the United States

www.ojp.usdoj.gov/nij

Issues in
International Crime

U.S. Department of Justice
Office of Justice Programs

810 Seventh Street N.W.

Washington, DC 20531

Alberto R. Gonzales
Attorney General

Regina B. Schofield
Assistant Attorney General

David W. Hagy
Deputy Assistant Attorney General, Office of
Justice Programs and Principal Deputy Director,
National Institute of Justice

This and other publications and products of the National Institute
of Justice can be found at:

National Institute of Justice
www.ojp.usdoj.gov/nij

Office of Justice Programs
Partnerships for Safer Communities
www.ojp.usdoj.gov

JAN. 07

Asian Transnational Organized Crime and Its Impact on the United States

This monograph is based on "Asian Transnational Organized Crime and Its Impact on the United States: Developing a Transnational Crime Research Agenda," final report to the National Institute of Justice, November 2004, NCJ 213310, available from the National Criminal Justice Reference Service at www.ncjrs.org/pdffiles1/nij/grants/213310.pdf.

Findings and conclusions of the research reported here are those of the authors and do not reflect the official position or policies of the U.S. Department of Justice.

Support for this research was provided by contract number TDL#1700–215 from the National Institute of Justice.

NCJ 214186

ABOUT THIS REPORT

The National Institute of Justice, as part of its effort to build an international research agenda that will help the United States better understand potential threats from transnational crime, supported this project to—

■ Determine high priority areas for research on Asian transnational organized crime.

■ Assess the impact of Asian transnational organized crime on the United States.

■ Identify relevant data and information sources in Asia.

■ Identify potential collaborative research partners and institutions in Asia.

This report focuses on the first two project goals.

What did the researchers find?

There is little consensus among Asian authorities as to what their main organized crime problems are. Further, Asian and U.S. interview participants had differing opinions about the importance of Asian transnational crime. The U.S. authorities viewed several offenses, including drugs, arms, and human trafficking, as serious problems that affect interests of the United States and undermine the stability of its Asian allies. Asian respondents generally tended to view "traditional" organized crime activities— such as extortion, gambling, loan sharking, prostitution, debt collection, and violence—committed by local and regional groups as a higher priority than transnational crimes.

Respondents in this study characterized the transnational organized crime networks operating in the region as highly specialized, with any overlapping of criminal activities occurring mostly at the level of transportation of goods and people. Contrary to the views of some U.S. authorities, the commonly expressed view among the study respondents was that there is no linkage between transnational organized crime groups and terrorist groups.

Preface

This study was undertaken on behalf of the National Institute of Justice between July 2003 and August 2004. Its purpose was to preliminarily assess the impact of Asian transnational organized crime on the United States while, at the same time, determining high-priority areas for further research and identifying potential collaborative research partners and sources of relevant data and information in Asia. The aim was thus not to examine the organized crime situation in the region in detail, but rather to lay the foundation for a research agenda that would ultimately accomplish this purpose.

A variety of techniques were used as part of the overall exploratory methodology. These included 4 months of interviews and field observations with experts including law enforcement officials, policymakers, and scholars, as well as U.S. officials, in eight Asian sites. Meetings were also held with Asian crime experts in the United States. Interviews and site visits were supplemented with surveys and analysis done by local Asian researchers, an analysis of U.S. indictments, and the review of a large volume of literature. The sites covered by the research are Cambodia, China, Hong Kong, Japan, Macau, the Philippines, Taiwan, and Thailand.

The first chapter of this monograph describes the divergent perceptions of Asian transnational organized crime held by the Asian versus the U.S. interview participants and also offers a researcher's perspective. The second chapter explains the scope and patterns of Asian organized crime. The final chapter offers an initial assessment of the impact of Asian transnational organized crime on the United States.

Contents

James O. Finckenauer and Ko-lin Chin

Introduction

By the late 20th century, organized criminal groups throughout the world were able to exploit the same economic liberalization, technology advances, and open borders that enabled multinational corporations to grow and prosper. Today, organized crime is a transnational phenomenon—and a cause for worldwide concern.

Transnational crime groups may have profited more from globalization than legitimate businesses, which are subject to domestic and host country laws and regulations. Transnational crime syndicates and networks, abetted by official corruption, blackmail, and intimidation, can use open markets and open societies to their full advantage.

As part of its effort to build an international research agenda that will help the United States better

About the Authors

James O. Finckenauer, Ph.D., is Distinguished Professor of Criminal Justice at Rutgers University and former director of NIJ's International Center.

Ko-lin Chin, Ph.D., is a Professor in the School of Criminal Justice at Rutgers University.

DEFINITION OF TERMS

This study uses the definition of an organized crime group that was established by an ad hoc committee of United Nations member states working on a convention to facilitate the prevention and combating of transnational organized crime:

"A structured group of three or more persons existing for a period of time and acting in concert with the aim of committing one or more serious crimes or offen[s]es in order to obtain, directly or indirectly, a financial or other material benefit."

According to the convention, an offense is transnational if—

1. It is committed in more than one state.

2. It is committed in one state but a substantial part of its preparation, planning, direction, or control takes place in another state.

3. It is committed in one state but involves an organized criminal group that engages in criminal activities in more than one state.

4. It is committed in one state but has substantial effects in another state.

STUDY METHODS

To achieve the multiple purposes of this project, researchers pursued several paths of inquiry:

■ **Interviews.** On three separate visits to Asia—together comprising about 4 months—researchers interviewed people familiar with organized crime in that part of the world. Altogether, they interviewed 139 subjects, including 61 Asian law enforcement officials, 30 U.S. officials (e.g., Federal Bureau of Investigation legal attachés, Drug Enforcement Administration representatives, immigration and customs officials, resident legal advisors for a U.S. embassy and consulate, and secret service personnel), 27 professors/researchers, 13 nongovernmental organization (NGO) workers, 6 persons engaged in commercial sex acts (i.e., prostitutes, exotic dancers, and other employees) or owners of sex establishments (such as brothels, sex clubs, and massage parlors), and 2 reporters. In addition, researchers spoke with law enforcement officials from the FBI and the U.S. Department of Justice's Organized Crime and Racketeering Section in Washington, D.C., who are dealing with organized crime matters and with staff in the Office to Monitor and Combat Trafficking in Persons at the U.S. Department of State.

■ **Field visits.** Researchers participated in a police raid of a sex club in Taipei, visited a detention center for illegal immigrants outside Taipei (where they interviewed two young Chinese women detainees), talked extensively to local residents of a leading migrant-sending community in China, and toured some crime hot spots accompanied by other U.S. or local authorities.

■ **Surveys.** Researchers asked a select number of experts in Beijing, Taipei, and Hong Kong to complete a survey instrument on organized crime in their respective jurisdictions and to prepare brief analyses on two illegal markets—drug trafficking and human smuggling and trafficking.

■ **Collection and analyses of documents.** Researchers examined 11 indictments involving Asian crime groups in the United States and a large volume of both the English and Chinese literature on Asian organized crime. They also had unique access to the original data from two studies undertaken by Ko-lin Chin (one of this report's two investigators): a recently completed study on the social organization of human smuggling groups and an ongoing project on the drug trade in Southeast Asia's Golden Triangle. These two studies involved interviews with hundreds of human smugglers and drug growers, producers, and traffickers.

understand potential threats from transnational crime, the National Institute of Justice (NIJ) supported a project to preliminarily assess organized crime in eight Asian countries or administrative regions (Cambodia, China, Hong Kong, Japan, Macau, the Philippines, Taiwan, and Thailand); pinpoint research issues of mutual interest to U.S. and Asian researchers; identify potential research partners (and their affiliated institutions) in Asia who might work collaboratively on these issues; and locate indigenous data sources that would be accessible to U.S. investigators.

For the most part, this monograph focuses on the project's preliminary assessment and provides a framework for the issues associated with transnational organized crime in Asia. Interested readers may obtain the full report, which is available on the National Criminal Justice Reference Service Web site at www.ncjrs.org/pdffiles1/nij/grants/213310.pdf.

Chapter 1

In the Eye of the Beholder: Perceptions of the Problem

What are the most serious problems associated with organized crime in the eight study sites? The answer to that question depends on who is asked. U.S. officials, whether in Asia or Washington, D.C., responded differently than Asian authorities, and even among the latter group, opinions varied according to jurisdiction.

The U.S. authorities who were contacted viewed several offenses (including drug, arms, and human trafficking) as serious problems that affect interests of the United States and undermine the stability of its Asian allies.

Asian respondents, broadly speaking, tended to view "traditional" organized crime activities (such as extortion, gambling, loan sharking, prostitution, debt collection, and violence) committed by local and regional groups as a higher priority than transnational crimes. The following section offers a brief country-by-country summary of the major organized crime issues and problems perceived by Asian authorities.

Asian Authorities' Perspective

Cambodia

The two leading organized crime problems in Cambodia are drug production/trafficking and human trafficking. Cambodian officials are concerned that drugs produced in neighboring countries are being trafficked into Cambodia for local consumption. Drug traffickers also use Cambodia as a transit country, but Cambodian authorities are less alarmed by this. The trafficking of Cambodian women into Thailand for sexual activities and the presence of a large number of Vietnamese women in Cambodia who are engaged in prostitution are major concerns for nongovernmental organizations (NGOs) in Asia. According to NGO representatives in Cambodia, however, local authorities are reluctant to crack down on the local commercial sex trade because they want to promote Cambodia as a place for cheap sex to attract tourists.[1] Some NGO personnel believe that Cambodian authorities are either directly involved in

the sex trade or benefit from it. These same sources indicate that there is no link between terrorism and human trafficking in Cambodia.

China

For Chinese authorities, the gravest organized crime problems, in order of seriousness, are:[2]

■ **Drug distribution.** The government is alarmed by the dramatic increase in the number of heroin addicts in China, and authorities believe that local and foreign-based drug syndicates are importing heroin from the neighboring Golden Triangle area and distributing it throughout the country (see "Drug Production and Trafficking in the Golden Triangle").

■ **Gambling and prostitution.** After being nearly eradicated following the 1949 communist takeover in China, gambling and prostitution are now thriving.

■ **Violence.** Crime groups are becoming better armed and more violent, and Chinese authorities are concerned about violent acts committed by mobsters against

rival gang members, ordinary citizens, business owners, and government authorities.

As for the future, according to Chen Xiao-cun of the Criminal Investigation Division, Ministry of Public Security, even more serious problems may lie ahead:

Our main concerns are that: (1) organizations with an underworld nature will penetrate into the legitimate business sector, (2) gangsters will get involved in politics and run for public office, and (3) they will eventually hook up with foreign-based organized crime groups.

Evidence suggests that many crime groups in China have already monopolized certain wholesale businesses and that the majority of these groups are protected by local authorities known as baohusan, or "protecting umbrella." In general, official corruption is seen to be a large and growing problem in China. Organized crime is a municipal, local, or regional (rather than national or transnational) phenomenon. Given the pace of economic development in China, and the interest of external investors in this

DRUG PRODUCTION AND TRAFFICKING IN THE GOLDEN TRIANGLE

The focal point of illicit drug production and trafficking in Southeast Asia is known as the Golden Triangle, a rugged, mountainous region that overlaps the borders of Burma (Myanmar), Laos, and Thailand. Although the tri-border region accounts for the majority of heroin production in Southeast Asia, the amount of heroin produced in the area has decreased by approximately 70 percent in the past 5 years. In 2004, Burma and Laos accounted for nearly all heroin produced in the region. Eradication efforts and the enforcement of poppy-free zones have combined to depress cultivation levels.

However, the decline in heroin production is being offset by an increase in the production of amphetamine-type stimulants (ATS). Methamphetamine is cheaper and easier to produce than heroin; it entails a simple process that starts with ephedrine, the principal alkaloid of ephedra, a shrub that grows wild on vast expanses of the nearby Chinese province of Yunnan.

Much of the heroin produced in the Golden Triangle reaches markets through southern China, although increased law enforcement pressure by Chinese authorities has forced some traffickers to seek new routes through Thailand. In Laos, the Mekong River is a major conduit for heroin trafficking and is patrolled in only a few areas. Many key drug areas, particularly in the north, are virtually inaccessible to Laotian officials. According to Interpol, "ethnic Chinese traffickers control the heroin trade in Oceania (often with Vietnamese criminal organizations), Malaysia, and the few remaining markets in Canada and the United States."

Hong Kong's position as a key port city and its proximity to the Golden Triangle and mainland China have made it a natural transit point for heroin moving from Southeast Asia to global markets. Although the amount of heroin transiting through Hong Kong appears to be diminishing, drug traffickers continue to use it as a base of operations.

development, the involvement of criminal organizations has significant implications, including a potential chilling effect on economic growth.

Tens of thousands of Chinese men and women are smuggled abroad each year to be laborers or to be sexually exploited. The arrival of large numbers of undocumented Chinese persons for these purposes is a cause of major concern in many countries.[3] Nonetheless, Chinese authorities do not consider this to be an organized crime problem—

or even a Chinese problem, because most snakeheads (human smugglers) are Chinese-Americans.[4] Local authorities noted the many benefits of having large numbers of their own people working abroad and sending money home. Indeed, study researchers observed considerable new housing development that is being fueled by money allegedly sent home by illegal workers in the United States.

Hong Kong

Hong Kong was a British colony for more than 100 years before it returned to Chinese control in 1997. It is now a special administrative region—meaning that it has a degree of autonomy—although that status is in constant contention with the mainland. Hong Kong has long been home to the secretive, ritualistic criminal organizations known as triads.[5] Authorities have a strong history of combating these triads—and of battling corruption as well—and the jurisdiction is widely known for its sophisticated and well-resourced police operations.[6] At the same time, Hong Kong is subject to much illicit movement of goods, services, and

people to and from the mainland. U.S. Drug Enforcement Administration (DEA) representatives in Hong Kong reported that some 18 million tons of cargo (both legal and illegal) destined for the United States pass through the port of Hong Kong in a year—a situation that clearly poses a security concern for the United States.

According to the elite Organized Crime and Triad Bureau (OCTB) of the Hong Kong Police, the leading organized crime problems in Hong Kong are car theft and smuggling, human smuggling, cross-border organized crime involving China and Macau, money laundering, drug trafficking, debt collection, and triad monopolies. Triad societies control private bus routes, fish markets, street markets, wholesale markets, entertainment centers, parking services, prostitution, illegal gambling, and extortion. In addition, each of the three triads (the Wo Shing Wo, the San Yee On, and the 14K) is said to be involved in the manufacture and street-level distribution of pirated VCDs and DVDs.

As a major transportation and financial center of Asia and a transit point in and out of

China, Hong Kong has been a hub for transnational organized crime activities for the past 30 years. Although triad organizations are active in Hong Kong, the OCTB indicated that no international triad organization exists. DEA representatives in Hong Kong said that drug trafficking was not well organized at the wholesale level. Instead, small groups of individual entrepreneurs serve as wholesalers, and the triads are mostly involved in organizing the street-level retail drug business.

Authorities interviewed said that the triads "are not interested in involving themselves in politics." The kinds of political/ideological missions associated with terrorism are said to be outside the ambitions or interests of the Hong Kong triads.

Japan

In Japan, the most serious organized crime problems are almost always related to the notorious Japanese organized crime groups—the yakuza.[7] Japanese authorities are mostly concerned with yakuza involvement in gambling, prostitution, amphetamine trafficking, and the victimization of legitimate businesses. According to Chief Seijirou Ikegami of the Anti-Organized Crime Division, Ueno Police Department, Tokyo Metropolitan Police, Japanese officials are also alarmed by the presence of a large number of legal and illegal immigrants from China (mostly Shanghainese, Fujianese, and Northeasterners) who are involved in organized crime activities and considered to be heavily armed and dangerous.

Because of its wealth and the spending power of Japanese businessmen, Japan has become a major destination country for women from Thailand, the Philippines, Colombia, China, Korea, and several other countries. In addition to women from abroad, Japan has a large number of local Japanese women who are involved in the sex industry.[8] Japanese authorities are convinced that yakuza members are heavily involved in the transportation and control of foreign persons for sexual purposes, but they do not view this as their most serious organized crime problem because (1) they believe these persons are not being forced into their activities, and (2) the Japanese public has not pressured authorities to do something about it.

Macau

Macau, a former Portuguese colony, is, like Hong Kong, a special administrative region of China. Macau aspires to be a tourist mecca and is dominated by gambling casinos, prostitution, and drugs. According to Sio-chak Wong, director of the Judiciary Police of Macau, the two major organized crime problems in Macau are gambling and illegal immigration/prostitution. Gambling is dominated by triad groups transplanted from Hong Kong, while illegal immigration/prostitution is controlled by crime groups formed by mainland Chinese. Recently, these Chinese crime groups began to be involved in fraud, money laundering, and the smuggling of stolen goods from Macau to China.

Because the Macau administration relies heavily on taxes from gambling—and prostitution is considered to be an important adjunct to the gambling industry—Macau authorities are reluctant to crack down on crime groups involved in these activities. As a result, organized crime groups maintain a strong presence in the gambling business in Macau. At the same time, Macau's commercial sex establishments are booming because of the arrival of large numbers of prostitutes from China.

The Philippines

Because of political instability and corruption, the country's economy is in disarray, which results in large numbers of Filipino people having to go overseas to work. Many of them are women, and a significant percentage of these women leave with an "entertainer visa" and end up being sexually exploited abroad.[9] Although the Philippine government has recently passed an anti-trafficking law, few human traffickers have ever been prosecuted and punished (see "Trafficking in Persons Report"). But Filipino officials are less concerned with the problem of Filipino persons engaged in prostitution abroad than with high-profile crimes such as drug trafficking, kidnapping for ransom, hijacking, bank robbery, prostitution, illegal gambling, and firearms smuggling.

The trafficking of amphetamine (called shabu in the Philippines) from China to the Philippines has been a major concern of Filipino authorities

TRAFFICKING IN PERSONS REPORT

The International Labour Organization (ILO)—the United Nations agency charged with addressing labor standards, employment, and social protection issues—estimates that 12.3 million people throughout the world are enslaved in forced labor, bonded labor, sexual servitude, and involuntary servitude at any given time. Millions of these victims are trafficked within their own national borders. According to the State Department's 2005 *Trafficking in Persons (TIP) Report*, approximately 600,000 to 800,000 men, women, and children are trafficked across international borders each year; of these, about 80 percent are female, and up to half are minors. The majority of transnational victims are trafficked into commercial sexual exploitation.

Tier Ranking System

The *TIP Report* evaluates the performance of 150 countries in terms of their compliance with the minimum standards of the Trafficking Victims Protection Act (TVPA) of 2000 (reauthorized in 2003 and 2005). Tier 1 countries are deemed to be in full compliance. Tier 2 countries are not in compliance but are making significant efforts to become so. Tier 3 countries are not compliant and are not making significant efforts toward that end. A Tier 3 assessment could trigger the withholding of certain types of U.S. aid.

The 2003 reauthorization of the TVPA created a Tier 2 Watch List of countries that warrant special scrutiny. The list consists of countries whose rating changed from the previous year's *TIP Report* or countries listed as Tier 2 in the current report where—

- The absolute number of victims of severe forms of trafficking is very significant or significantly increasing.

- There is a failure to provide evidence of increasing efforts to combat severe forms of human trafficking from the previous year—including increased investigations, prosecutions, and convictions of trafficking crimes; increased assistance to victims; and decreasing evidence of complicity by government officials.

- The determination that a country is making significant efforts to bring itself into compliance with minimum standards was based on commitments by the country to take additional future steps over the next year.

Since trafficking likely extends to every country in the world, the omission of a country from the *TIP Report* may only indicate a lack of adequate information.

The TVPA defines severe forms of trafficking as "(1) sex trafficking in which a commercial sex act is induced by force, fraud, or coercion, or in which the person induced to perform such an act has not attained 18 years of age; or (2) the recruitment, harboring, transportation, provision, or obtaining of a person for labor or services, through the use of force, fraud, or coercion for the purpose of subjection to involuntary servitude, peonage, debt bondage, or slavery."

Status of the Eight Sites in This Report

Of the eight sites that researchers visited, only Hong Kong was considered fully compliant with the minimum requirements of the Trafficking Victims Protection Act of 2000. Japan, Taiwan, and Thailand were assigned Tier 2 rankings, and Macau (due to insufficient information) was not listed at all.

(continued on page 12)

TRAFFICKING IN PERSONS REPORT (CONTINUED)

Two countries—China and the Philippines—were put on the Tier 2 Watch List. In the case of China, this designation is due to its failure to provide evidence of increasing efforts to combat trafficking (specifically, its inadequate protection for trafficking victims—especially foreign women and Chinese women deported from Taiwan). The Philippines was placed on the watch list because, despite widespread allegations of law enforcement complicity in trafficking, the Government reported no prosecutions of trafficking-related corruption. The Government made "modestly better efforts" during the performance period to implement its 2003 anti-trafficking law, i.e., it dedicated four state prosecutors to focus on trafficking-related cases and provided training to law enforcement officials. The 2005 *TIP Report* indicates that "28 cases are currently under investigation" and that "at least 15 cases are being

prosecuted under the anti-trafficking law and other statutes . . . . [But] corruption and a weak judiciary remain serious impediments to the effective prosecution of traffickers."

Cambodia, a source, destination, and transit country for men, women, and children trafficked for the purposes of sexual exploitation and forced labor, was assessed as Tier 3 for its lack of progress in combating severe forms of trafficking, particularly its failure to convict traffickers and public officials involved in trafficking. In addition, the Government failed to take effective action during the performance period to ensure that those responsible for a raid on an NGO shelter for trafficking victims (which included removal of several victims) were held accountable and brought to justice. In short, Cambodia's anti-trafficking efforts remained hampered by systemic corruption and an ineffectual judicial system.

TIP Report Assessment of Eight Countries

Country	Tier 1	Tier 2	Tier 2 Watch List	Tier 3	Inadequate Information
Cambodia				X	
China			X		
Hong Kong	X				
Japan		X			
Macau					X
Philippines			X		
Taiwan		X			
Thailand		X			

for a long time. Recently, many shabu laboratories have been established in the Philippines, in part because of the improved effectiveness of tighter coastal patrols in stopping the drug flow from abroad. Authorities indicated that the drug business in the Philippines is controlled by predominantly Filipino-Chinese, or Chinese from China, Hong Kong, and Taiwan who are protected by local politicians.

A U.S. Government official interviewed in Manila said that organized crime and terrorism in the Philippines are separate activities. The terrorists are said to be isolated groups and not involved in such transnational crimes as human trafficking and drug smuggling. A Filipino official indicated that some terrorist groups may be involved in kidnapping for ransom, but they do not play a major role in such crimes because their numbers are not strong in Manila, where most of the wealthy Chinese (who are potential victims) live.

Taiwan

In Taiwan, the number one organized crime problem is heijin, the penetration of

mobsters into the legitimate business sector and the political arena.[10] Many influential gangsters in Taiwan are now chief executive officers of major business conglomerates, and they are heavily involved in the businesses of bid-rigging, waste disposal, construction, cable television networks, telecommunications, stock trading, and entertainment. Further, starting in the mid-1980s, many criminals have successfully run for public office in order to protect themselves from police crackdowns.

In addition to heijin, Taiwanese authorities are concerned with traditional organized crime activities such as gambling, prostitution, loan sharking, debt collection, extortion, and gang violence. Kidnapping for ransom is also a serious concern; influential and wealthy figures are often targeted and, as a result, a large number of Taiwanese entrepreneurs have departed for a safe haven abroad.

A relatively recent and growing transnational crime problem is the production and distribution of pirated CDs and DVDs. Each of the three major criminal gangs surveyed in

Taiwan is said to be involved in this business. Another transnational crime—drug trafficking—was cited as a problem but considered less worrisome to authorities than human smuggling. Even though Taiwan is a destination country for heroin from the Golden Triangle and amphetamine from China, Taiwanese authorities are more concerned with the influx of prostitutes (or potential prostitutes) from China, who are smuggled into Taiwan by boats across the Taiwan Strait or arrive through fraudulent marriages with Taiwanese citizens.[11]

At the time of this study, one detention facility was holding more than 1,000, mostly young, Chinese women awaiting deportation back to mainland China, some for as long as 9 months. Taiwanese law enforcement authorities were frustrated by dealing with uncooperative Chinese authorities on this issue. Also frustrating them were rulings of Taiwanese judges who do not consider human trafficking to be an organized crime problem and thus do not apply the country's anti-organized crime laws to the networks engaged in these activities.

As in mainland China, respondents in Taiwan reported no concerns about any possible connections between organized crime groups and either terrorist groups or so-called armed opposition groups.

Thailand

The two leading organized crime groups in Thailand are the jao phor (godfathers) and the United Wa State Army (or the Red Wa).[12] Jao phor are mostly ethnic Chinese based in the provinces who have business interests in both legitimate and criminal activities. Moreover, they have groups of associates and followers; move closely with powerful bureaucrats, policemen, and military figures; sit in positions in local administration; and play a key role in parliamentary elections. According to Thai authorities, jao phor groups reside in 39 of Thailand's 76 provinces. The United Wa State Army is also a major concern for the Thai government because this organization, located in the Burmese part of the Golden Triangle, is believed to be responsible for manufacturing and trafficking millions of methamphetamine tablets (called yaba or mad drug in Thailand) into the

country for local consumption. Although heroin produced by the Red Wa and other groups in the Golden Triangle continues to pass through Thailand, Thai authorities are less concerned with this drug because the country's local heroin market is relatively small.

Thailand is also a source, transit, and destination country for trafficked women,[13] but Thai officials are not concerned by the sizeable presence of Burmese women engaged in prostitution in their country or by the trafficking of Thai women to Japan and Europe to be sexually exploited. Because prostitution is vital to the country's enormous tourist industry and Thai policemen are believed to be heavily bribed by sex establishment owners, authorities do not consider the illegal sex industry to be an organized crime problem.

U.S. Authorities' Viewpoint

As already noted, U.S. authorities are much more likely than their Asian counterparts to consider transnational organized crime activities to be the more

serious organized crime problems in Asia. This could be explained by differing focuses of the two groups, or might be attributable in some cases to lack of knowledge and understanding of the local situation by the Americans as a result of having to depend on outside sources for information. In any event, from the U.S. viewpoint, the problems of drug production and trafficking, human smuggling, trafficking in women and children for the purpose of prostitution, arms trafficking, and money laundering are all very serious problems in Asia. Americans interviewed also thought these activities have either a direct or indirect impact on U.S. interests or, at the very least, that they have undermined the stability and well-being of ally countries in Asia.

None of the Americans interviewed believes that terrorist groups and transnational organized crime groups are linked. (As previously indicated, this is the view held by some of the Asian authorities as well, among those who expressed any opinion on the issue.)

Researchers' Vantage Point

Contrary to the opinions of many in U.S. law enforcement, this study found that the relationship between traditional organized crime groups (such as the triads and the yakuza) and transnational crime is tenuous. Asian authorities in China and Hong Kong indicated that human smuggling, for example, is carried out primarily by loose networks or "mom and pop" groups with no ties to organized crime—a claim borne out by data from personal interviews with such smugglers. This difference in understanding about who is engaged in transnational crime may account for some of the disparity in priorities between criminal justice agencies in the East and West. Another difficulty has to do with what constitutes transnational crime. As discussed earlier, Asian authorities may be reluctant to treat certain transnational activities as crime because they are beneficial to the local economy, and the people who are involved may not be gangsters or professional criminals. Such perceptual and communication problems pose challenges for collaborative research but are not insurmountable.

Based on the interviews, fieldwork, and literature review conducted as part of this project, the five leading organized crime problems in Asia (not necessarily ranked in the order presented here) are (1) drug production and trafficking, (2) trafficking in women and children, (3) human smuggling, (4) the links among organized crime/ politics/official corruption, and (5) the penetration of organized crime into legitimate businesses. For research purposes, it is recommended that funding be targeted to the first three problems (detailed below) because of the inevitable obstacles that U.S. researchers would face in trying to study criminal infiltration into politics and business—areas that, in any event, do not affect the United States directly. It is further recommended that research efforts be both bilateral (principally with China) and multilateral in nature. The full report identifies a wide variety of potentially willing research partners and assesses their strengths and weaknesses.

- **Drug production and trafficking.** Traffickers are taking advantage of China's open-door policy and using the land route from the Golden Triangle to distribute heroin both to markets inside China and to ports where it can be shipped to other countries. This enables them to move hundreds of kilograms in one delivery and helps them develop a huge market as they wend their way through a country with more than 1.3 billion people. In addition, large quantities of this heroin may reach the United States.

  Massive quantities of methamphetamine produced in the Golden Triangle are trafficked to Thailand. The explosion of methamphetamine use in Thailand has caused a serious internal problem and also exacerbated existing hostility between Thailand and Burma, thus worsening a volatile international situation. Amphetamine production in China has caused a problem of its use there, and trafficking of amphetamine to Taiwan, Japan, and the Philippines has created problems for those countries.

- **Trafficking in women and children.** This human rights problem, which affects many thousands of victims, is getting worse rather than better. Research is needed to differentiate between trafficking and smuggling, and their respective consequences, to put to rest claims made by Asian law enforcement that women cross borders voluntarily to increase their income, and to remove the emotionalism surrounding this issue—as reflected in terms such as "sex slave" and "debt bondage."

- **Human smuggling.** In some ways, this is a more serious problem than human trafficking because of the numbers involved (millions, not thousands). In addition, smuggling fees per person have increased from about $30,000 in the early 1990s to $65,000 after the events of September 11, 2001. Smuggling has a direct impact on the United States because many illegal aliens end up in America.

Chapter 2

Scope and Patterns of Organized Crime

Many crime groups exist in Asia, some of them indigenous and others imported from abroad or formed by foreigners. As with the task of ranking the seriousness of organized crime problems in Asia, an attempt to generalize the scope of each and every organized crime group is difficult because this may depend on the country, the group, and the product or service involved.

Scope

In general, most traditional organized crime groups (i.e., mafia-like criminal organizations in China, organized gangs in Taiwan, triad societies in Hong Kong and Macau, and jao phor in Thailand) are local in scope. Three Chinese organized crime syndicates identified in a recent U.N. study—the Liu Yong Syndicate, the Zhang Wei Syndicate, and the Liang Xiao Min Syndicate—were all said to be local or at most regional in their scope, and to be without cooperative relationships with other organized crime groups.[14]

No doubt, some members of such local/regional organizations may have influence at the national level, but their legal and illegal operations are more likely to be local in nature. An exception is the yakuza in Japan. A Japanese official said in an interview that yakuza members are very much involved in the trafficking of persons and the operation of sex establishments in Japan, and some members of these various crime groups may also travel to other countries or may be involved in bilateral or multinational criminal activities. However, they, and the members of other Asia-based organized crime groups, are not key players in transnational criminal activities.[15]

A Chinese official in Beijing (referring to mafia-like crime groups known in China as "black societies") explained the organized crime/transnational crime connection this way: "According to our law, there are four types of organized crime groups: (1) criminal groups; (2) criminal organizations; (3) black

society-like criminal organizations; and (4) black societies. At this point, we don't yet have black societies, but we expect them to be formed in the very near future. The [other] above-mentioned three groups are not involved in transnational crime. That is because these groups are all territorial—their spheres of influence and their activities are restricted to their own turfs. They are not mature enough to establish a transnational crime network." Similarly, assessments of specific criminal organizations in Taiwan do not indicate any involvement on the part of these groups in transnational crime. A drug market analysis in Taiwan, however, showed that some organized crime groups may be active in the transnational trafficking of new, synthetic drugs.

In the Philippines, interview participants said specifically that the transnational "headhunters" who recruit people for prostitution there are not members of organized crime groups. And, a Thai official stated: "In Thailand, there are influential groups [organized crime groups] and there are transnational organized groups formed by foreigners. There is not much relationship existing between the influential groups and the transnational organized crime groups."

Even those nontraditional organized crime groups that are heavily involved in transnational crimes such as drug trafficking and human smuggling/trafficking are local or at most national in scope. Their transnational criminal operations are almost always compartmentalized. Most large-scale transnational criminal activities, such as the trafficking of hundreds of kilograms of heroin or the smuggling of hundreds of illegal immigrants, involve numerous independent groups operating in source, transit, and destination countries. There are also, however, "mom and pop," small-scale transnational criminal activities involving, for example, a couple trying to smuggle a small amount of drugs or two or three migrants from one country to another. What is unique about transnational crime is that it can be carried out in some cases by an individual (e.g., computer crime) or by a group or network with hundreds of members or associates.[16]

Specialization

Most of the study subjects suggested that there is little specialization among traditional organized crime groups. Most of these groups are involved in a variety of both legitimate and illegitimate businesses. While these crime groups continue to be involved in traditional organized crime activities such as gambling, prostitution, drug distribution, loan sharking, debt collection, and violence, they are also expanding their influence into legitimate businesses such as the stock market, construction, waste disposal, wholesale markets, and the food industry.

However, according to the study subjects, transnational crime networks are highly specialized. It is relatively unlikely for a human smuggling organization to be involved in drug trafficking, or for a drug-manufacturing group to participate in the trafficking of women for prostitution.

The only overlapping or non-specialization that may occur is among offenders who are involved in transportation. In this instance, individual members, as opposed to crime groups as a whole,

may cross over in providing services for smuggling and trafficking. Even though different groups operate each transnational criminal activity in the source and destination countries, and these various groups do not get involved in more than one type of transnational crime, the same group responsible for transportation (e.g., a boat captain and crew) may simultaneously be involved in smuggling both drugs and human beings.

Structure or Opportunity?

Traditional organized crime groups are longstanding, preexisting groups, while transnational crime networks are developed in response to current criminal opportunities. Some of the traditional organized crime groups mentioned above have been in existence in Asia for centuries and they are most likely to continue to exist. These groups have names, structure, territory, and a strong attachment to their environment, and as a result are handicapped in taking advantage of criminal opportunities that are transnational in nature.[17] The second group, the networks of transnational

crime, are more likely to emerge around specific opportunities. Very often, a nuclear or an extended family will initiate an operation in response to a new opportunity and people from the same village or at least the same ethnic group who are living in source, transit, and destination countries will be recruited to participate as members of a network that may dissolve after the criminal operation is successfully carried out.

This distinction has implications for both research and policy. For research, there is a need to expand the current thinking about the causes of organized crime and about the risks and vulnerabilities that may lead to the creation of criminal markets. There is also a need to better understand how those criminal markets operate in order to provide useful information to shape strategies and tactics to disrupt them. For policy, law enforcement officials need to do more thinking "out of the box" of traditional, mafia-like structures in order to effectively combat the crime networks that are dominating transnational organized crime.

The Flow

There are several major movement patterns involving people who are sexually exploited, drugs, and laborers on the transnational scene.

Prostitutes. In Asia, the most notable flows of trafficked women are (1) from the Philippines to Japan, (2) from Thailand to Japan, (3) from Burma (Myanmar) to Thailand, (4) from Vietnam to Cambodia, and (5) from Nepal to India. There are also somewhat less notable movements such as (1) from Cambodia to Thailand, (2) from Laos to Thailand, and (3) from the Philippines to Korea.

The most significant development in human smuggling and trafficking, however, is the massive movement of women from China to other Asian countries and, indeed, to the rest of the world. Authorities in all the countries visited indicated that many Chinese women are showing up in their sex industries; sex establishments in Hong Kong, Taiwan, Macau, and Japan have almost been taken over by Chinese women. The presence of large numbers of Chinese

women in the sex industries of Burma, Thailand, Singapore, Malaysia, Indonesia, Australia, and the United States has also been heavily reported.

Drugs. In Asia, heroin is produced in the Burmese part of the Golden Triangle and flows into the international market via either Thailand or China. China's heroin market is expanding rapidly, and heroin markets exist in most Southeast Asian countries and also in Australia. Methamphetamine also is produced in the Burmese part of the Golden Triangle; Thailand is the main market for the drug. It is smuggled into Thailand either across the Burma-Thai border or through Laos and Cambodia. Amphetamine is mainly produced in China and smuggled into Taiwan, Japan, the Philippines, and other Asian countries.

Undocumented workers. A large number of Chinese laborers are smuggled by boat into Taiwan across the Taiwan Strait. Chinese are also arriving in Japan and Burma in large numbers. The presence of a substantial number of Chinese, both legal and illegal migrants, is a matter of concern for the majority of nations in Asia. Undocumented workers are also a matter of concern in the United States.

Chapter 3

Impact on the United States

The following discussion does not deal with the garden variety of crimes that just happen to have been committed in the United States by Asians, nor the Asian street gangs that operate in certain U.S. cities. Instead, the focus is on those crimes that appear to be transnational in nature— the United States being on the receiving end—and that originate in (or at least involve) any of the eight countries (or administrative regions) that were the focal point of the study.

Further, impact and harm are construed broadly here, to include not only direct criminal activities in the United States, but also harm and/or potential harm to U.S. interests both at home and abroad. For example, given the history and the volatility of relations between mainland China and Taiwan, and the strong U.S. interest and investment in that area, criminal developments involving those entities are of critical interest to the United States. In other cases, where there are developing U.S. business interests, such as in China and in the casino industry in Macau, again there is the potential for a criminal impact on U.S. interests.

Additionally, a word about methodology is necessary. As noted, principal respondents in the interviews were nationals (scholars, law enforcement officials, and in some cases victims) of the respective countries that were visited. Thus, their perspectives of how what they know might impact the United States are pretty much speculative. Even in the cases of the U.S. officials that were interviewed in each country, their perspectives on the crime and organized crime problems are an "in country" view, albeit keeping U.S. interests very much in mind.

In addition to the interviews and field visits that were conducted, local scholars in Hong Kong and Taiwan prepared market assessments of the criminal markets of human trafficking and drug

trafficking and analyses of the major organized crime groups in each of their respective areas. It should be recognized that these reflect the perspectives of the native scholars.

None of this should be construed to mean that the interviews, assessments, and analyses are not valuable—quite to the contrary. The original sources provided a foundation, a stepping-off point, to compare and relate what was learned from them with a plethora of existing secondary materials. The latter include in particular:

■ The U.S. State Department's *Trafficking in Persons (TIP) Report* for 2004.

■ "Sex Trafficking of Women in the United States" (a 2001 report to NIJ by Janice Raymond and Donna Hughes).[18]

■ "The Commercial Sexual Exploitation of Children in the U.S., Canada, and Mexico" (a 2002 report to NIJ by Richard Estes and Neil Weiner).[19]

■ "Survey of Practitioners to Assess the Local Impact of Transnational Crime" (a 2003 report to NIJ by Abt Associates).[20]

■ *Blood Brothers: The Criminal Underworld of Asia* by Bertil Lintner (2002).[21]

Threat, Impact, and Harm to the United States

When asked about transnational crime, only a few of the Asian respondents referred to specific crimes impacting the United States. For example, according to members of the faculty of the Fuzhou Police College in China, the principal forms of transnational crime involving China and the United States are kidnapping and human trafficking. Officials of the Bureau of Investigation of the Ministry of Justice of Taiwan stated that fake IDs are used to gain Taiwanese passports for travel to the United States by Chinese who are being smuggled here. But these are not seen as high priority (or even medium priority for the most part) problems in Asia. On the other hand, human trafficking and smuggling were indeed high-priority issues for most of the U.S. authorities interviewed. These included U.S. officials both in Washington and abroad. For instance, an FBI official indicated that such activities as trafficking in

women/children who are sexually exploited, trafficking in human beings for the purpose of labor, and illegal immigration were transnational criminal activities of Chinese organized crime groups in the United States.

Human trafficking is one problem for which there is a seemingly vast difference in priority and perspective between Asian and U.S. authorities. The Asian authorities view what is happening in the transnational movement of people as mostly smuggling. People wanting to leave China, for example, pay smugglers to transport them to Taiwan or even to the United States. There is little or no coercion or deception in these cases. This is part of the reason for the Asian authorities' lack of concern.

The Asian experts interviewed also do not see this smuggling as an activity of traditional organized crime groups. A top criminal investigator with the Ministry of Public Security in Beijing told researchers that human trafficking was indeed "organized," but that it was not a form of organized crime. He indicated the main destination countries for Chinese women were Japan, Korea, Russia, Taiwan, and Hong

Kong. A correspondent in Hong Kong indicated that none of the three most prominent organized crime groups in Hong Kong (the San Yee On, the Wo Shing Wo, and the 14K) are involved in human smuggling or human trafficking. Other authorities in Hong Kong likewise said that there is very limited trafficking in Hong Kong, that the vast majority of people moving transnationally are smuggled (not trafficked), and that this is a "mom and pop" industry not controlled by organized crime. These views reflect those of authorities in the other locations visited as well. For example, representatives of the National Police Administration in Taiwan said there is no evidence of human smugglers engaging in other transnational organized crime activities, nor are they involved with well-established organized crime groups. In fact, as previously noted, because the judges in Taiwan do not consider human smuggling to be an activity of organized crime, they do not enforce the Organized Crime Prevention Law against smugglers.

So what is the impact of Asian human smuggling/trafficking on the United States? Both the United Nations and the United

States (in the Department of State's annual *TIP Report*) make much of the connection between organized crime and human trafficking. The 2004 *TIP Report* concludes that trafficking fuels organized crime. As indicated above, interviews conducted for this study and examination of the data from the *TIP Reports* seem to belie that claim—at least as far as the specific problem of smuggling/trafficking from Asia to the United States is concerned.

Some empirical evidence sheds light on the issue. The Raymond and Hughes study[22] tracked incidents of trafficking to the United States between 1990 and 2000. Of 38 specific cases they described, 18 had an Asian connection, particularly from Thailand or elsewhere in Southeast Asia. From the brief descriptions of these cases, some are clearly alleged to have organized crime involvement, but a dozen or so cases over a 10-year period does not seem to be a very large number. Further, Raymond and Hughes's interview respondents in the 2001 study indicated that the trafficking organizations with which they were familiar were mostly small, having only one to five people involved. This supports a "mom and pop" characterization rather than one of organized crime.

So what does a typical mom-and-pop case look like? The "News Item" is illustrative.

NEWS ITEM

U.S. Federal authorities arrested in Miami a husband and wife team who allegedly smuggled thousands of Chinese illegal immigrants into the United States over the past 20 years. Alexandre Wei, a Taiwanese national with French citizenship, and his wife Bing Xei, a Chinese citizen, used Miami, Florida, as the U.S. entry point for their clients, who usually ended their round-the-world journey in New York City. In Manila, U.S. and Philippine authorities arrested the couple's son Jacques, a suspected co-conspirator, along with six other Chinese. This family of people smugglers would first send their clients from China to the Philippines and several other Asian countries. They would then be moved to France, Suriname, or the French territories in the Caribbean, Jamaica, or the Bahamas. From the West Indies, the illegal immigrants were moved to Florida. The illegal immigrants were charged as much as $50,000 each by the smuggling ring.

—Tanya Weinbert,
Sun-Sentinel (Fort Lauderdale, Florida),
November 11, 2003

The Estes and Weiner study[23] surveyed a variety of sources, including 1,000 informants in 17 U.S. cities, in an examination of the commercial sexual exploitation of children (including trafficking). The study concluded that among the "less common" forms of this exploitation was participation by international organized crime networks. Only 10 percent of the children they encountered had been trafficked internationally, and that included from all sources (Africa, Central and Latin America, and Central and Eastern Europe) not just from Asia. Thus again, these findings do not support a belief that human trafficking to the United States by Asian organized crime is a major problem.

In its survey of 184 State and local police departments from across the United States, Abt Associates[24] asked how many had conducted investigations and made arrests for human trafficking (which was among a list of transnational crimes they asked about). The sources of the trafficking were not delineated, but fewer than a third had conducted investigations, and fewer than a quarter had made arrests in any instances

of human trafficking. Extrapolating from this to how much of their activity may have involved Asian organized crime, this would again seem to produce relatively small figures.

A review of recent Federal indictments involving all forms of Asian organized crime supports the point further. A request to the Organized Crime and Racketeering Section of the U.S. Department of Justice produced 11 Racketeer Influenced and Corrupt Organizations (RICO) indictments of Asian criminals for a variety of crimes in the United States. The indictments covered the period 1993 to 2002. (These were not all the cases involving Asian organized crime, nor a representative sample of all the cases. Instead, they are simply an opportunity sample.)

Seven of the eleven indictments charged crimes that could be construed to be related to human trafficking, e.g., interstate travel for illegal sexual activities, prostitution, kidnapping and hostage taking, asylum fraud, and alien smuggling. Perhaps the best known of these cases is the "Sister Ping" case. Chen Chui Ping, who is referred to

as "the mother of all snake-heads," allegedly earned $30 million over 15 years transporting thousands of undocumented Chinese people into the United States. To do so, she retained subcontractors in New York and other United States cities. These included the notorious Fuk Ching gang in New York, who performed the domestic chore of transporting smuggled Chinese from Boston to New York City. Apart from this connection with a known criminal group, Sister Ping and her operation very much exemplify an entrepreneurial criminal network as opposed to a transnational organized crime group.

Keeping in mind the proviso about representativeness above, the first general observation that can be made is that seven such cases over a 10-year period again does not appear to be an especially large number. Secondly, an examination of the details in the indictments indicates that most of these cases involved crimes that were indeed organized by opportunistic networks, e.g., Sister Ping, and not by traditional and well-defined Asian organized crime groups having the characteristics outlined previously. This reinforces the earlier

observation that it is the opportunistic, rather than the organized, crime groups who are the key players in Asian transnational crime.

That the transportation of human beings across borders is a smuggling rather than a trafficking issue, that it is conducted by entrepreneurial criminal networks rather than by traditional organized crime, and that the estimates of victims and cases may be overstated does not mean that there is no reason for concern. There are current estimates that some 11 million illegal immigrants are living in the United States. No one knows how many of these may be Asian. What can be assumed, however, is that any substantial number affects United States resources. Demands on education, health care, and social services and for jobs have a financial impact. This point is reflected in a study visit to a village near Fuzhou in China that has been the source of much smuggling of people to the United States. There, 35 to 40 Chinese children of preschool age were referred to by an official guide as "citizens," as in U.S. citizens. They were children born in the United States, now being raised in China until they

reach school age, at which point they will return to the United States for schooling. The costs of educating these children—many of whom have parents who were illegal immigrants—will obviously have a financial impact on the United States.

Impact on Broader U.S. Interests

Irrespective of how much crime emanating from Asia may actually show up on United States shores, broader United States interests are at stake here. These interests relate to humanitarian concerns, to business interests, to political relationships, to investments in training and assistance, and to law enforcement cooperation.

The United States does, and very much should, have an interest in what happens to trafficking victims and to persons who are being smuggled across national borders. This interest exists apart from the question of how many such persons actually end up in the United States. It is a humanitarian and human rights issue. As elsewhere in the world, the problem in Asia requires effort and investment on both the demand

and supply sides of the human trafficking/smuggling equation. Economic development and opportunity must be coupled with action to combat exploitative sex tourism, corruption, and official indifference.

U.S. business interests in Asia include casinos in Macau and trade in China and Taiwan. To the extent that the local and regional organized crime in these countries penetrates, interferes with, and jeopardizes business, it is harmful to U.S. interests. A specific example of this sort of harm is the crime of intellectual property theft, including software piracy. All six of the criminal organizations surveyed in Taiwan and Hong Kong, for example, are reported to be involved in pirated CDs and DVDs. In the case of the Wo Shing Wo, it is said to be the dominant activity in which the group is involved. A U.S. customs official interviewed in Beijing stressed the problem of intellectual property theft as a major concern.

As elsewhere, the United States has made a considerable investment in law enforcement training and assistance in Asia. The United States, for example,

operates the International Law Enforcement Training Academy in Bangkok that has trained hundreds of law enforcement operatives from throughout the region. It is obviously in the best interests of the United States to see this investment pay off, which would lead to more effective combating of the crime problems described herein. With respect specifically to drug trafficking, the DEA emphasized in the course of this study that China is a critically important player on the Asian drug scene; it was described as the key to heroin trafficking. What is needed, according to the DEA, is more joint investigative training and exchanges of intelligence information between the United States and China.

The United States must balance politically its interests in China, Hong Kong, and Taiwan. Because the crime problems covered by this study are, for the most part, regional problems, they require regional solutions. It is in the U.S. interest to play the role of honest broker in helping the region deal with organized crime.

Finally, a number of law enforcement officials, particularly in Taiwan and China, expressed dissatisfaction with Interpol and with cooperation from U.S. law enforcement. Interpol is regarded as basically ineffective. With respect to U.S. cooperation, the officials complained of essentially being ignored when they made requests for information and assistance. The Mutual Legal Assistance Treaty system was criticized as involving too much "red tape." Whatever the merits of these complaints, they obviously have implications for U.S. efforts to secure information and assistance for its own investigations.

Conclusion

The National Institute of Justice has recognized that crime and criminals more and more have a global face. This recognition means expanding NIJ's international research agenda to both better appreciate and to better understand potential threats from transnational crime. This preliminary assessment of Asian organized crime, including the pinpointing of potential research issues of mutual interest and the identification of potential research partners in Asia, lays a solid foundation for that expanded research agenda.

Notes

1. Gilboa, Amit, *Off the Rails in Phnom Penh: Into the Dark Heart of Guns, Girls, and Ganja,* Bangkok: Asia Books, 2001.

2. He Bingsong, *Organized Crime in China,* Beijing: China Legal Press, 2002 (Chinese language publication).

3. Smith, Paul, ed., *Human Smuggling,* Washington, DC: Center for Strategic and International Studies, 1997; Kwong, Peter, *Forbidden Workers: Illegal Chinese Immigrants and American Labor,* New York: The New Press, 1997; Emerton, Robyn, "Trafficking of Women Into Hong Kong for the Purpose of Prostitution: Preliminary Research Findings," Occasional Paper No. 3, Hong Kong: University of Hong Kong, 2001; Brazil, David, *No Money, No Honey!: A Candid Look at Sex-for-Sale in Singapore,* Singapore: Angsana Books, 2004.

4. Chin, Ko-lin, *Smuggled Chinese: Clandestine Immigration to the United States,* Philadelphia: Temple University Press, 1999.

5. Chu, Yiu-kong, *Triads as Business,* London: Routledge, 2000.

6. Lo, T. Wing, *Corruption and Politics in Hong Kong and China,* Buckingham: Open University Press, 1993.

7. Hill, Peter, *The Japanese Mafia: Yakuza, Law, and the State,* New York: Oxford University Press, 2003; Kaplan, David, and Alec Dubro, *Yakuza: Japan's Criminal Underworld,*

Berkeley: University of California Press, 2003.

8. Kaplan and Dubro, *Yakuza: Japan's Criminal Underworld* (see note 7).

9. Santos, Aida, *Patterns, Profiles and Health Consequences of Sexual Exploitation: The Philippine Report,* Manila: Coalition Against Trafficking in Women, 2002.

10. Chin, Ko-lin, *Heijin: Organized Crime, Business, and Politics in Taiwan,* Armonk, NY: M.E. Sharpe, 2003.

11. Chang Tseng-liang, "A Study on the Problem of 'Fake Marriage' Across Taiwan Strait, Focusing on Fake Marriage for the Purpose of Prostitution," *Central Police University Journal of Police Science* 33 (1) (2002): 203–236 (Chinese language publication).

12. Phongpaichit, Pasuk, and Sungsidh Piriyarangsan, *Corruption and Democracy in Thailand,* Chiang Mai: Silkworm Books, 1994.

13. Asia Watch, *A Modern Form of Slavery: Trafficking of Burmese Women and Girls Into Brothels in Thailand,* New York: Human Rights Watch, 1993; Brown, Louise, *Sex Slaves: The Trafficking of Women in Asia,* London: Virago Press, 2000; Jeffrey, Leslie Ann, *Sex and Borders: Gender, National Identity, and Prostitution Policy in Thailand,* Chiang Mai: Silkworm Press, 2002.

14. United Nations Centre for International Crime Prevention, "Overview of the 40 Criminal Groups Surveyed," *Trends in Organized Crime* 6 (2) (2000): 131–135.

15. Chu, Yiu-kong, *Triads as Business* (see note 5); Hill, Peter, *The Japanese Mafia: Yakuza, Law, and the State* (see note 7); Zhang, Sheldon, and Ko-lin Chin, "The Declining Significance of Triad Societies in Transnational Illegal Activities," *British Journal of Criminology* 43 (3) (2003): 463–482.

16. Zhang, Sheldon, and Ko-lin Chin, "Enter the Dragon: Inside Chinese Human Smuggling Operations," *Criminology* 40 (4) (November 2002): 737–768.

17. Zhang and Chin, "The Declining Significance of Triad Societies in Transnational Illegal Activities," 463–482 (see note 15).

18. Raymond, Janice, and Donna Hughes, "Sex Trafficking of Women in the United States," final report for the National Institute of Justice, grant number 98–WT–VX–0032, 2002, NCJ 187774.

19. Estes, Richard, and Neil Weiner, "The Commercial Sexual Exploitation of Children in the U.S., Canada, and Mexico," final report for the National Institute of Justice, grant number 1999–IJ–CX–0030, 2002, NCJ 195561.

20. Abt Associates, "Survey of Practitioners to Assess the Local Impact of Transnational Crime," final report for the National Institute of Justice, contract number 99–C–008 T005, Washington, DC, December 2003.

21. Lintner, Bertil, *Blood Brothers: The Criminal Underworld of Asia*, New York: Palgrave McMillan, 2002.

22. Raymond and Hughes, "Sex Trafficking of Women in the United States" (see note 18).

23. Estes and Weiner, "The Commercial Sexual Exploitation of Children in the U.S., Canada and Mexico" (see note 19).

24. Abt Associates, "Survey of Practitioners to Assess the Local Impact of Transnational Crime" (see note 20).

The National Institute of Justice is the
research, development, and evaluation
agency of the U.S. Department of Justice.
NIJ's mission is to advance scientific research,
development, and evaluation to enhance the
administration of justice and public safety.

NIJ is a component of the Office of Justice
Programs, which also includes the Bureau
of Justice Assistance, the Bureau of Justice
Statistics, the Office of Juvenile Justice
and Delinquency Prevention, and the
Office for Victims of Crime.

PRESORTED STANDARD
POSTAGE & FEES PAID
DOJ/NIJ
PERMIT NO. G-91

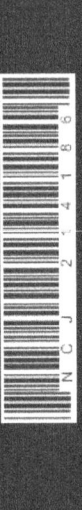

MAILING LABEL AREA (5" x 2")

DO NOT PRINT THIS AREA

(INK NOR VARNISH)

U.S. Department of Justice
Office of Justice Programs
National Institute of Justice

Washington, DC 20531

Official Business
Penalty for Private Use $300

www.ingramcontent.com/pod-product-compliance
Lightning Source LLC
Chambersburg PA
CBHW080617180526
45168CB00007B/2947